DREAM TEAM

PHOTO CREDITS

David Leah/Allsport USA: Cover; Larry Bird, Clyde Drexler,
Patrick Ewing, Magic Johnson, Christian Laettner, Karl Malone,
Scottie Pippin, David Robinson and John Stockton.
Pgs., 2/3, 10, 16, 20, 22, 24 and 28.
Noren Trotman/Sports Photo Masters: Cover; Charles Barkley,
Michael Jordan and Chris Mullin. Pgs. 6, 8, 12, 14, 18, 26 and 30.

Library of Congress Cataloging-in-Publication Data
Available upon request.

ISBN 1-56766-050-9

DREAM TEAM

by Richard Rambeck

Magic Johnson, Michael Jordan,
and David Robinson played like a dream
for the U.S. during the Olympics.

It's Just A Dream Team Isn't It?

There had never been a team like this one, except in the dreams of U.S. basketball fans. What if all the top pro stars in the United States played together on the same squad at the same time? Imagine. Magic Johnson would lead the fast break. On Magic's right would be Charles Barkley. On Johnson's left would be Michael Jordan. What would Magic do? Pass it to Barkley for a monster slam dunk? Or would he give it to Jordan and let Michael fly over the defenders for a graceful jam? Or would Magic fake it to both Barkley and Jordan and then throw a no-look pass to Larry Bird for a three-point shot? Imagine. It's a dream, isn't it?

Well, the dream came true in the summer of 1992. The United States sent its best professional players—its Dream Team—to Barcelona, Spain, to compete in the Summer Olympics. The Barcelona Games marked the first time that the U.S. pros could play in the Olympics. In the past, the United States had to send teams made up of top college players to international competitions such as the Olympics, the Pan American Games, and the World Basketball Championships.

In 1992, though, the world saw the best players in the United States playing in the

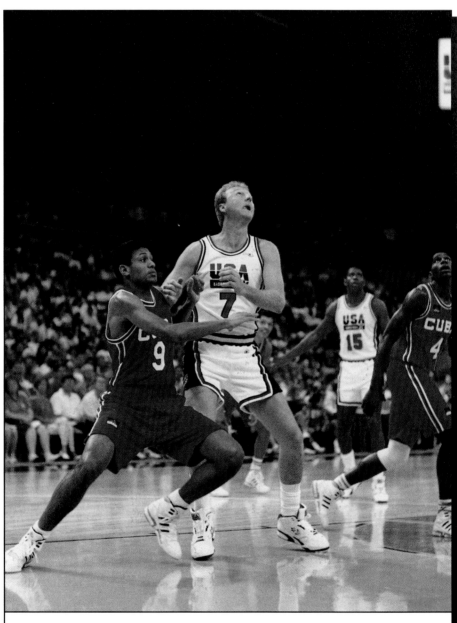

Larry Bird had back problems,
but the Boston Celtics star scored
nineteen points in the victory over Germany.

Olympics. The world saw some of the brightest stars in the history of the game of basketball: Michael Jordan, Magic Johnson, Larry Bird, Charles Barkley, David Robinson, Patrick Ewing, and others. The U.S. squad was known as the Dream Team, but it proved to be a nightmare for opponents in the Olympics. The Americans played eight games in Barcelona. The "closest" game for the U.S. came in the game for the gold medal. The United States won by thirty-two points. The Dream Team left no doubt that most of the best players in the world are from the U.S.

Letting The Best Into The Olympics

There really was never any doubt that the United States would claim the men's basketball gold medal in 1992. In fact, the 1992 gold medal was probably won by the U.S. in 1989. That's when the International Basketball Federation, known as FIBA, voted to open the Olympic Games to all players, even those in the National Basketball Association. "We, of course, know the U.S. will win everything for the time being," said Boris Stankovic, general secretary of FIBA. "But we also think that the only way other countries can improve is by playing against the best."

Other nations had already improved a lot, as

Patrick Ewing won his second gold medal in 1992;
he was a member of the
1984 U.S. Olympic Team.

the popularity of basketball grew all over the world. The U.S., which had lost only one Olympic game from 1936 to 1984, could no longer win major international competitions with teams made up of college stars. The U.S. finished second in the 1987 Pan American Games, third in the 1988 Olympics, second in the 1990 Goodwill Games, third in the 1990 World Championships, and third in the 1991 Pan American Games. But it would be a different story at the 1992 Olympics, because for the first time the top pros in the United States would be playing.

Or would they? Would these NBA stars want to go to the Olympics, which took place during what is usually the basketball offseason? The answer was yes. Not a single NBA star said he didn't want to play in Barcelona. After all, national pride was at stake. But which of the many NBA stars would be on the team? Would there be tryouts? USA Basketball, which is this country's governing body of the sport, decided the team would be picked without holding tryouts.

USA Basketball chose longtime NBA coach Chuck Daly to be the head coach. Then, in September 1991, a USA Basketball committee

David Robinson, who played on the
1988 U.S. Olympic Team that wound up third,
got the gold this time.

picked ten of the twelve players who would be on the team. The other two, including one college star, would be chosen several months later. The first ten members of the Dream Team included some of the best ever to play the game. Point guard Magic Johnson of the Los Angeles Lakers, guard Michael Jordan of the Chicago Bulls, and forward Larry Bird of the Boston Celtics were the easy choices. The Dream Team also included two centers, Patrick Ewing of the New York Knicks and David Robinson of the San Antonio Spurs.

Also selected were forwards Scottie Pippen of the Bulls, Karl Malone of the Utah Jazz, and Charles Barkley of the Philadelphia 76ers. (Barkley was later traded to the Phoenix Suns.) Rounding out the first ten were guards John Stockton of Utah and Chris Mullin of the Golden State Warriors. In the spring of 1992, two more players were added: guard Clyde Drexler of the Portland Trail Blazers and forward Christian Laettner, who had just finished his college career and had led his Duke team to two straight NCAA titles.

The Dream Team was complete, but some of the players nearly didn't make it to Barcelona for the Olympics. Magic Johnson was forced to

Scottie Pippen held Croatia star guard
Toni Kukoc to four points
in the first game between the teams.

retire from the Lakers in November 1991 after testing positive for the virus that causes AIDS. Magic said, however, that he would play for the Dream Team. "Anyone who really knows me has never had a question about me being there," he said. "I don't want there to be any doubt. I am ready." Larry Bird missed much of the Celtics' season with a bad back, but the Boston star was ready when the Dream Team started practicing in June 1992.

The twelve Dream Teamers finally came together at the University of California at San Diego for five practices. At first, there was some concern that it would be impossible for Chuck Daly to get a team of superstars to pass the ball to each other. After a couple of workouts, Daly said the Dream Team's problem was that the players were passing too much. "Once they adjust to each other, they'll be fine," Daly said.

The Dream Team had to qualify for the Olympics by finishing in the top four at the ten-team Tournament of the Americas, which was held in Portland, Oregon, in late June and early July. But nobody was expecting the Dream Team to lose in Portland. "Don't even think about that. It cannot happen," said

John Stockton (shown here with his children)
had injury problems,
but he still played in the Olympics.

Renato Brito, president of the Brazilian Basketball Federation. "I don't think the United States will have any trouble beating the rest of us."

Brito was right. The U.S. won all six games it played in Portland, defeating Cuba 136-57, Canada 105-61, Panama 112-52, Argentina 128-87, Puerto Rico 119-81, and Venezuela 127-87. The Dream Team was as good as, or better than, expected. "I've been in the NBA something like fifteen years now," Daly said, "and I still marvel at some of the things these people are capable of doing—things that you'll never see again. We are seeing the greatest players in the history of the game."

The Dream Team's biggest problem in Portland was staying healthy. Patrick Ewing dislocated a thumb, John Stockton suffered a minor break in his leg, Larry Bird's back started bothering him again, and Clyde Drexler sat out a game because of a strained knee. Stockton missed the last four games of the Tournament of the Americas, and Bird played little except in the first game. But the injuries didn't slow down the Americans a bit.

"We're playing the way we should," Bird said. "If we get it going in Barcelona, I don't

17

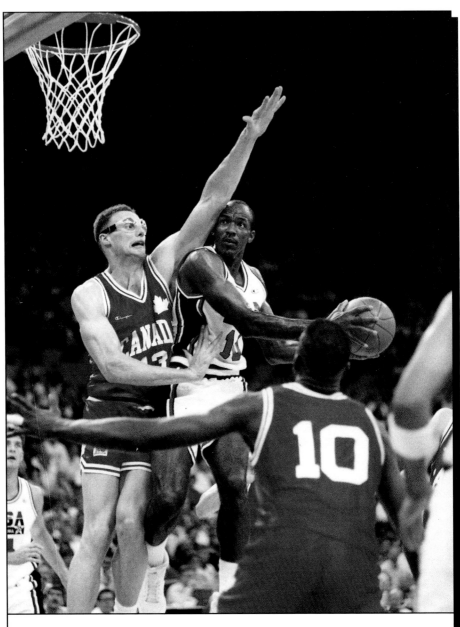

Clyde Drexler wasn't one of the
top scorers for the Dream Team,
but he played well in every game.

think there's any team that can stay with us. When this team gets going and its defense is clicking, we could beat these teams by whatever. Eighty, ninety to a hundred points maybe." Julio Toro, coach of Venezuela, agreed with Bird. "The U.S. is 200 light-years ahead of the rest of the world," Toro explained. "You could take an all-star team of all the other teams in this tournament, give us a thirty-point lead and the ball, and we'd still lose."

Once the Dream Team reached Barcelona, players from other nations admitted they had little hope of beating the Americans. "They should just give the U.S. the gold medal and get it over with," said Dino Radja, a forward for Croatia, one of the top teams in the Games. "The United States is going to win every game in the Olympics by twenty-five or thirty points," said Radja's teammate, Toni Kukoc. "And if the Americans have a bad day, maybe they'll win by only fifteen."

The Dream
Comes True
At The
Olympics

The Americans did not have a bad day in their opening game in Barcelona, which was against African champion Angola. The Angolans got off to a good start, actually leading the U.S. 2-1 and pulling into a 7-7 tie after a three-point shot. But then the Dream Team lived up to its

Magic Johnson hurt his knee against Germany,
but returned three games later
to run the U.S. offense.

superstar billing. The U.S. scored the next thirty-one points before Angola hit a free throw to make the score 38-8. Then the Dream Team outscored the Africans 15-0 to take a 53-8 lead. The halftime score was 64-16. The final was 116-48.

While fans were talking about all the dunks and easy layups the U.S. scored, the Dream Teamers were talking about other parts of their game. "Coach Daly has stressed if we can play tough defense and rebound, the offense will take care of itself," said Magic Johnson, who had six points and ten assists. "You see us out there shooting layup after layup—the reason for that is our defense." While everyone played defense for the U.S., Charles Barkley (twenty-four points) and Karl Malone (nineteen) provided much of the offense.

In the Dream Team's second game, against Croatia, Magic Johnson hurt his knee midway through the first half and had to be carried off the court. Johnson's injury left the U.S. without a true point guard because John Stockton hadn't yet recovered from his broken leg. Despite the injuries, Croatia was no match for the Americans. Led by Michael Jordan's twenty-one points and eight steals and

Charles Barkley, the top scorer for the Dream Team,
sparked the U.S. in the
gold medal game against Croatia.

Barkley's twenty points, the U.S. rolled to a 103-70 victory. Johnson's injury was serious enough to keep him out of the next two games, but the Americans weren't concerned. "This team can play without a lot of people," Johnson said.

The U.S. played without both its point guards in the next game, which was against Germany. But Michael Jordan stepped nicely into the role, and the Dream Team never lost a step, beating the Germans 111-68. Jordan scored fifteen points, dished out twelve assists, and didn't make a single turnover. The U.S. also got an outstanding game from Larry Bird, who finally seemed to be free of his back trouble. Bird, who hardly played in the first two games, scored nineteen points.

U.S. Finishes First Round Undefeated

The U.S. ended the first round of play by defeating Brazil 127-83 and then Spain 122-81. Charles Barkley led the way against both Brazil (thirty points) and Spain (twenty). The Dream Team, which finished at the top of its six-team first-round group with a 5-0 record, moved on to the quarterfinals to play Puerto Rico. Puerto Rico had defeated the U.S. at the 1991 Pan American Games. This time, however, there would be no Puerto Rican upset.

Chris Mullin, the Dream Team's
top three-point shooter, had twenty-one points
in the win over Puerto Rico.

Led by Larry Bird's seven points, the Dream Team jumped out to a 17-0 advantage as Puerto Rico missed its first twelve shots. The Puerto Ricans didn't give up, though, as the tiny Caribbean nation scored the next thirteen points. But the Dream Team was just too much. Chris Mullin, Magic Johnson, and Scottie Pippen each hit a pair of three-point shots in the first half, leading the Americans to a 67-40 halftime lead. The U.S. wound up winning 115-77. Mullin led the way for the Dream Team with twenty-one points. David Robinson scored fourteen, Magic Johnson thirteen, and Pippen twelve. Christian Laettner added eleven points and a team-high eight rebounds.

The talented Dream Team then moved into the semifinals to face Lithuania, which defeated Brazil 114-96 in the quarterfinals. But the Lithuanians weren't expecting to beat the Dream Team and advance to the championship game. "I think we have no chance," said Lithuania point guard Rimas Kurtinaitis. "We're ready to play for third place." Despite Kurtinaitis' opinion, Lithuania, which until recently was a republic that was part of the Soviet Union, had a strong squad. Four of the

Karl Malone, known as the Mailman,
delivered for the U.S.
by scoring nineteen points against Angola.

Lithuanian stars were starters on the Soviet Union team that defeated the U.S. in the 1988 Summer Olympics.

The 1992 U.S. squad had a lot of respect for Lithuania. "There was a sense of competition, so that was a challenge to this team," Michael Jordan explained. The Dream Team answered the challenge, routing the Lithuanians 127-76. Led by Jordan, the U.S. raced to an 11-0 lead. After Lithuania pulled to within 14-8, the Dream Team scored the game's next twenty points. At that point, with the Americans leading 34-8, Jordan had outscored Lithuania by himself, 12-8. Jordan led the Dream Team with twenty-one points. Karl Malone added eighteen, Magic Johnson had fourteen points and eight assists, and David Robinson chipped in thirteen points and eight rebounds.

The Dream Is Completed Against Croatia

The victory over Lithuania moved the U.S. into the game for the gold medal. The Dream Team played Croatia, a squad the Americans had already defeated by thirty-three points in the Olympics. Croatia, a nation that until recently was part of Yugoslavia, gave the Dream Team its toughest game in the Olympics. Led by six-foot-ten guard Toni Kukoc and back court mate Drazen Petrovic,

Christian Laettner had eleven points
and a team-leading eight rebounds
in the quarterfinal against Puerto Rico.

the Croatians rallied after trailing 14-4 to take a 25-23 lead midway through the first half.

Croatia's advantage lasted one trip down the court, as Charles Barkley hit a three-point shot to put the U.S. ahead 26-25. Croatia trailed the rest of the game. Barkley scored ten points as the Dream Team extended its lead to 56-42 at halftime. In the second half, Michael Jordan took over, scoring fourteen of his team-high twenty-two points. Led by Jordan, the U.S. went on an 11-0 run to take an 80-53 lead with twelve minutes to go in the game. The Croatians battled hard, but couldn't get closer than twenty-five points the rest of the way. The final score was 117-85.

After the game, when the U.S. players were given their gold medals, the Spanish fans cheered as if the Dream Team were their own heroes. They cheered for Michael Jordan and Scottie Pippen, for Patrick Ewing and David Robinson, for Chris Mullin and Clyde Drexler, for John Stockton and Karl Malone, for Larry Bird and Christian Laettner. And for Charles Barkley, who was the Dream Team's leading scorer during the Olympics. But the loudest cheer was for Magic Johnson, who came out of retirement to play for the Dream Team. "This

Michael Jordan, filling in at point guard
against Germany, had
fifteen points and twelve assists.

is the best," said Magic, who also had won five NBA titles and one NCAA championship. "This is bigger than all of them put together. This is for everybody in America."

Magic and his teammates came to Barcelona aiming to show the world that the best basketball is still played in the United States. Everybody, including players on other teams, expected the U.S. to win each game by at least thirty points. That's exactly what the Dream Team did. "We did what we were expected to do," Michael Jordan said. "Everybody back home can be proud of the way our team plays basketball." The way the U.S. played basketball at the 1992 Summer Olympics was like a dream. But this was one dream that came true.